The One Skill

The One Skill

*How Mastering the Art of Letting Go
Will Change Your Life*

Leo Babauta

WAKING LION PRESS

This book is written out of gratitude for my wonderful readers, who've been a constant source of encouragement and support over the years. It has meant more than I can express. Thank you.

ISBN 978-1-4341-0522-6

Published by Waking Lion Press, an imprint of the Editorium

Waking Lion Press™ and Editorium™ are trademarks of:

The Editorium, LLC
West Jordan, UT 84081-6132
www.editorium.com

The views expressed in this book are the responsibility of the author and do not necessarily represent the position of Waking Lion Press. The reader alone is responsible for the use of any ideas or information provided by this book.

Contents

Chapter 1

Why Letting Go

The root of all of our problems is our inability to let go.

I gleaned this idea from a book on Zen Buddhism one day a few years ago, and it struck me in its simplicity.

Could it be true?

Consider this idea: a bird in flight. The bird lives totally in the moment, completely focused on its flight, perhaps using its sharp eyes to search for food.

It doesn't start thinking, "Why does it have to be so cold here? What do the other birds think of me? What am I going to do when I meet up with the other birds later? Will I be successful at nest building? Why can't I have bigger breasts? Why can't I wake up earlier like the other birds?" And so on.

Of course, as humans we have bigger brains than the bird, and we can solve problems and create poetry and build skyscrapers. So we have lots more ability and lots more going on than the simple bird floating on the wind.

These bigger brains, though, cause us all the problems that we have. I don't mean the problems with poverty and disease, but the problems with overthinking things, feeling anxiety and frustration and depression and anger over the things that happen to us and might happen to us and have already happened to us but that we can't stop thinking about.

So I've been testing out this Zen idea in the last few years, and the results have been amazing: I've reduced my stress, started procrastinating less, improved my relationships, increased my ability to deal with change, learned to change difficult habits, and become more present in my life.

It's hard to overstate the case for the skill of letting go. And the resistance most people feel to the idea of letting go is just as great.

Let's take a few examples (I'll go into more detail in later chapters):

- **Stress:** Our stress comes from wanting things to be a certain way, and then we get stressed when things inevitably don't go that way. But if we could let go of how we wanted it to be, and accepted and appreciated reality as it is, we would let go of the stress.

- **Procrastination:** We procrastinate because of a fear of failure, hard tasks, confusion, discomfort. But if we could let go of wanting things to be easy, successful, comfortable . . . and just accept that there is a wide range of experiences, we could just do the task.

- **Habits & distractions:** By the way, most people have a hard time changing habits for this same reason—we procrastinate on the habit just like we procrastinate on work tasks. We also go to distractions all day long for the same reasons.

- **Irritation/frustration with people:** We get irritated with people because they don't behave the way we'd like. And this damages our relationships with them, because we're angry at them. It makes us less happy. Instead, we could let go of wanting them to be a certain way, accept them as they are, and just be with them. It makes the relationship much better—I've seen this with my dad, my wife, my kids.

- **Loss & death:** When a loved one dies, or we lose a job, or we get a major illness, this is a loss that causes grieving and suffering. And while that's unavoidable (and we should accept our grieving), being able to let go helps us to deal with this loss.

- **Being present:** Many of us would like to be more

present in life, so that we don't miss it as it happens, so that we can enjoy it fully. Imagine having a delicious dish in front of you, and you eat it but are thinking about work while you chew . . . you'd be missing out on the flavors of the dish. But if you could give it your full attention, you'd fully appreciate the dish. Life is exactly like this . . . we are so obsessed with thinking about other things, that we can't be present in the moment. We can learn to let go of this future- or past-oriented thinking, and be more present.

- **Fear:** The root of our problems is fear—from procrastination to not starting a business to being overweight—and the root of fear is holding onto how we want things to be. More on this later, but for now, it's enough to note that if we can let go of or loosen up on how we really want things to be, we can loosen up the fear as well.

That's just a taste, but you can start to see how letting go becomes an incredible skill that can make you better at dealing with all of life's problems.

And letting go is a skill that can be practiced. It's not easy, but it can be learned in a practice of just 5 minutes a day. Amazingly, this short 5-minute daily practice, as easy as it might seem, adds up to great things.

In this concise book, we'll look at how letting go

works with many types of problems, and how we can develop and practice the skill of letting go.

Chapter 2

Dealing with Procrastination

Everyone procrastinates, but why?

Out of fear: fear of failure, fear of something difficult or uncomfortable or confusing.

And where does this fear come from? An ideal: that we'll succeed, that things will be comfortable and fairly easy, that we'll know what we're doing.

Let's take the case of Nathan, who has a thesis paper to write. He's been putting this thesis off for months now. I know, he's probably the first person ever to put off a thesis paper.

What's stopping him? Well, it's a big overwhelming task, complicated and a bit confusing. He knows it will take days, even weeks to work on, and so it's built up a huge status in his head. He's not even sure where to start, and the thought of having to do all that tedious research and writing is scary. It's all scary. So the fear of all this makes his mind want to run to easier things, from reading things online to social media to watching TV shows.

Nathan's fear comes from an ideal that he doesn't even think about, but that's there nonetheless. The ideal is that life will be comfortable and easy. That he'll know what he's doing and feel competent and successful. When things don't meet up with this ideal, he avoids them.

When you have an ideal, you fear not meeting the ideal. You hold onto this ideal, and in your mind it becomes real.

So what can Nathan do about this ideal that's causing the fear that's causing the procrastination? How can he overcome all of this to get his thesis done?

He can let go of the ideal. Life doesn't have to be easy—in fact, the hard stuff is how we achieve anything of value. Life doesn't have to be comfortable—in fact, when we get out of our comfort zone, we grow. He doesn't have to know what he's doing—it's when we do things we don't know how to do that we learn new things, new skills, and get better at them.

He can be grateful for the difficulty that leads to achievement, the discomfort that leads to growth, the uncertainty that leads to learning.

He can let go of the ideal, and so it won't be so scary.

He can accept that things will be difficult and uncomfortable, embrace that, and do it anyway. He can be present with the task, and do it in this moment.

Let go, accept, embrace, be present, do. A cure for procrastination.

Chapter 3

Dealing with Fear

It's not just procrastination that's caused by fear—pretty much all of our problems are rooted in fear. With deeper roots in our ideals/ expectations/fantasies, as we saw in the last chapter.

Let's take a look at some other common problems caused by fear:

1. **Debt:** There are many possible causes, but often you're spending more than you make because of a shopping habit, or a fear of letting go of some of the comforts you're used to. The shopping habit might be caused by anxiety (fear that something you want isn't going to happen) or loneliness (fear that you're not good enough) or wanting your life to be better than it is (fear that you're not okay as you are). Letting go of comforts (like your morning Starbucks, or your nice house or car) can be

difficult if you fear discomfort, fear that you won't be okay if your life is less comfortable, fear that others will judge you if your house/ car/clothes aren't as nice.

2. **Relationship problems:** There are obviously lots of possible causes (including that the other person has major problems, though you should always look at yourself as well) . . . but some fears that cause relationship problems include fear of letting go of control (causing you to want to control the other person), fear that you're not good enough, fear of abandonment and other trust issues, fear of not being accepted, fear of accepting the other person (actually this is a fear of control problem).

3. **Can't exercise:** Again, lots of causes, but some of them include: not enough time (fear of letting go of something else that you're used to doing), exercise is too hard (fear of discomfort), distractions like TV and the Internet (fear of missing out, fear of discomfort).

4. **Can't change diet:** Same as exercise really. Although there are also often emotional issues, in which case the fears can be very similar to the ones that lead to the shopping habit and financial problems.

5. **Aren't doing work you love:** You maybe don't know what you want to do, which means you

haven't committed to really exploring (fear of failing), or you know but haven't taken the plunge (fear of failure), or fear that you're not good enough.

6. **Stressed about work/school:** You have lots to do, but the amount isn't the problem. The amount is an objective fact, and either you have enough time to do it (and perhaps do it well) or you don't. The real problem is that you're worried about getting it all done, which means you have an ideal (I'm going to get it all done on time, and it'll be done perfectly) and you fear that this ideal won't come true. So the fear is based on an ideal, but the ideal isn't realistic. You won't get it all done perfectly and on time. No one does. Accept the reality, that you'll get some done, to the best of your ability, and if you fail you'll learn from that, and that's how the world works. No one is perfect. The ideal doesn't exist in reality.

And so on. All other problems are some manifestation of what's going on in the above examples.

Fear of failure, fear of not being good enough, fear of letting go of control, fear of being alone, fear of abandonment, fear of discomfort, fear of missing out, fear that you're not okay as you are or your life isn't okay as it is, fear that some ideal won't come true.

These all stem from ideals, and a lack of trust in yourself, and in the present moment.

If we can practice letting go of the ideals, and start to accept and trust in ourselves and the present moment, then we can overcome lots of problems. Problems are rooted in fear, which is rooted in ideals. Let go of the ideals.

Chapter 4

Dealing with Difficult People

People can be frustrating, from rude drivers on the road to coworkers whose habits annoy you to kids who won't do what you ask them to.

And while I'm not saying we should just be happy with the horrible behavior of other people, letting go of how we want them to be can make us a lot happier.

Let's take Marie as an example: she's mad because her co-worker Scott snapped at her in anger and was very rude and insulting.

There's no excuse for Scott's bad behavior . . . but Marie responding in anger will not likely help the situation. Nor will dwelling on it angrily make Marie very happy.

There are a few things to note here:

1. Scott is probably having a bad day. Or is just not

good at dealing with stress, or expressing himself very well. Whatever the problem, it's rooted in the co-worker's issues, not with Marie. So she shouldn't take his actions personally—the rudeness and anger weren't really about her.

2. Even if Scott had a legitimate point to make about Marie (perhaps she did something wrong), he could have made the point calmly or constructively. He didn't, so while Marie might find the takeaway point (don't use Comic Sans for business reports), she doesn't need to read too much into his anger. He has an anger problem that's about him, not her.

3. Marie can and should respond to Scott, but responding in anger won't help. If she can let go of the anger response (which naturally comes up), she can respond calmly and constructively.

4. It's not Marie's responsibility to change Scott. She can't force him to be a nicer person, even if she tried. Instead, she can change her own response, which is her responsibility.

5. However, Marie can act compassionately here, even if she doesn't feel Scott "deserves it." What he deserves isn't at issue. If he's suffering, she can be the bigger person and try to be compassionate with his suffering (and her own). This will

improve the situation and possibly make them both happier.

Now, I realize that many people will dwell on what's "right" in this situation. Scott is in the wrong and deserves to be punished or corrected, but definitely shouldn't be given a pass or treated compassionately. This is the problem: our ideal about what is "right." There is no absolute right—that's just an ideal that we have. We have expectations that everyone act in the "right" way, but that's not going to happen in reality.

Holding onto our ideals of how everyone should act—which isn't reality—is what causes our anger, frustration, stress, disappointment. Instead, we can let go of those ideals, and accept the reality.

What's the reality? Scott is suffering, has anger issues, is stressed out about something, and acted badly. Marie can accept this, let go of her ideals and the resulting anger, and instead respond with compassion and calm. She can deal with Scott in an appropriate way, instead of acting out of anger in an inappropriate way.

Not easy, but letting go of ideals, accepting reality, and acting appropriately and with compassion can be practiced.

Chapter 5

Dealing with Distractions

Distractions are the flip side of procrastination—we don't want to focus on one thing, because it's uncomfortable or hard, and so we let ourselves go to distractions.

Those distractions are comfortable and easy. We're good at them. We don't have to fear them, fear failing at them, fear discomfort or uncertainty. From video games to online reading to social media to TV, distractions are where our minds want to run to.

So how do we deal with the pull of these distractions? Not surprisingly, we can practice letting go of them. Try this little letting go practice:

1. See what distraction you're going to, and what appeal it has for you. Perhaps it's validation, or a little dose of something interesting or entertaining. This appeal is what you're craving, why you're drawn to it.

2. Now see the disadvantages of this distraction. How is it hurting you?

3. See the impermanence of this distraction—it gives you a temporary pleasure, but not lasting happiness. You get a dose of pleasure but then need another dose immediately after, and so on, without end.

4. Try letting go of the distraction, just for a little while. Instead, practice being content with your life without the distraction. What in your distractionless life can you be grateful for?

5. What other sources of happiness can you find that are inside of you, rather than outside of you (like the distractions)? Can you be content with yourself? Can you enjoy the activity that's in front of you, such as reading a novel or writing something or spending time in nature?

6. See the freedom that arises from letting go of the distraction. This is a good thing.

This practice, in small bites, is not difficult. Try it now, for a few minutes. Then again in a little while. You'll get better with practice.

Chapter 6

Dealing with Habits

Building a new habit is fairly simple: you do the habit you want (let's say exercise) right after a trigger (let's say your morning coffee), and repeat that enough times that it becomes automatic. After awhile, when the trigger happens, the urge to do the habit automatically arises.

So why do we have such difficulty forming habits? It turns out that some things get in the way of this simple process:

- **Fear of doing the new habit.** Exercise & meditation are two good examples—people have fears about them (they're hard, uncomfortable, confusing, etc.) and so they avoid them and run to distractions instead.

- **Being tired or things coming up that get in the**

way. There are legitimate reasons not to do the habit. But if we're committed to the new habit, we can figure out solutions to these obstacles, like going to bed earlier or planning ahead to find a new time to do the habit if something will get in the way tomorrow. And so it's a learning process, but what really gets in the way is that we give up when we fail, because we have an ideal that we'll succeed immediately.

- **Old habits die hard.** When we start a new habit, we're changing an old habit. Exercise in the morning is replacing reading Facebook and blogs in the morning. So doing the new habit requires consciously letting go of the old habit and mindfully doing the new habit until it becomes more automatic and habitual.

Those are not insurmountable obstacles, but each one requires letting go of something:

1. Let go of an ideal that's causing the fear.

2. Let go of the ideal that we'll succeed immediately, and instead accept failure as part of the learning process, and consciously and continuously find ways to improve.

3. Let go of the old habit and mindfully do the new one instead.

And so the skill of letting go can help us mindfully form new habits.

Chapter 7

Dealing with Possessions

One of the best things I've done is decluttered my life, getting rid of a lot of junk and unnecessary possessions—from furniture to clothes to gadgets to tools to books to dishes to memorabilia and much more.

The uncluttered home is a thing of beauty and joy to me. But even more importantly, I learned about myself in the process of letting go of possessions.

Why had I accumulated so many possessions in the first place? It turns out that my family (including me) had a habit of impulse buying, and buying out of tradition. We also habitually acquire things without getting rid of old ones. We stuff things in storage to make room for new ones, and then forget about them.

But why was I holding onto them? A lot of the possessions were surprisingly easy to get rid of, but a lot of them were also very difficult to part with. I had emotional attachments to these items.

It turns out that they were serving emotional needs for me: they made me feel secure and safe, they gave me comfort, they gave me memories (and love), they were hopes that I had for the future (unread books, exercise and sports equipment). In truth, I didn't need these items for any of these emotional needs—I could meet those needs in other ways, without possessions.

And so letting go of possessions meant letting go of what I thought those possessions meant to me. It meant letting go of the self that I was when I had those possessions. It meant letting go of the life I had when those possessions were in my life.

It was a wonderful process, this letting go. It taught me that I was capable of living happily without things I thought were needs.

I taught me that letting go can be both painful and joyful, a process of loss and of liberation.

Chapter 8

Dealing with Resistance
from Others

Often we want other people to change, or we want to make a change but other people resist that change.

Why can't they just let go and accept the change? Because we can't force change on other people—we don't control them.

And so letting go becomes a process of accepting that we can't control other people, or even control much of the world. Life isn't something we control, no matter how much we try.

Let go of our illusion of control.

A good example of this is when you become a parent: at first, you seem to control your child's life completely, because you control their home and clothes and food and play. You think you are shaping this young child into the human you'd like them to be.

As they get older, this becomes very frustrating. They don't behave the way you'd like them to behave. They aren't interested in the hobbies you'd like for them. They don't always have the values you insist they adopt. They don't agree with much of what you say.

You want to control them, but they resist. It turns out, they're their own people. They are independent, individual people, and they'll grow into people they want to become. You have some influence on that, of course, but not control.

And it turns out, we never really had control in the first place. Even when they're babies and toddlers, we control their environment, but they decide how to internalize that, and different babies react differently. And we react to their reactions, so actually they're changing us just as much as we're changing them.

This is true of all people in our lives. We don't control them, and we can't. We can influence them. They influence us as well.

Let go of wanting to control people, of wanting to change them. Their resistance is natural. Instead, focus on yourself, and be the shining example. Be the compassionate center. See if you can help in ways that they find helpful.

Chapter 9

Dealing with Change

One of the truths that I've learned is that everything—every person, every situation, every object, every being—is impermanent.

We are not permanent beings. Even the self that we think we are is constantly changing—there's some continuity, perhaps, but not the same self. Everyone is like this.

Even objects that seem to stay the same are not. They're decomposing, getting older, fossilizing, getting weathered, getting fragile.

This impermanence is scary, and it's also liberating.

When we can see this impermanent nature in everything around us, in ourselves, in our lives . . . we can see that we've been grasping at nothing. It's like reaching up with your hands to grab the wind. And this grasping, this trying to hold onto something that's never the same, never staying still . . . this is why we're suffering. It's why we fear things, why we procrastinate and go to distraction, why we get stressed and angry and frustrated.

This constant change, this impermanence and the loss that goes with it (we're constantly losing our lives, losing ourselves as we know it) . . . this is scary. We want things to stay the same, and yet they never do. This is why we suffer.

So how can we deal with this fear of constant change and impermanence and loss? We can start by accepting it. It is the reality of life. We cannot change the impermanence of life or ourselves. We can fight against it and suffer, or we can accept it.

And we can see the freedom in this impermanence. If we are never staying the same, then yes, we are losing this safe idea of ourselves that stays the same . . . but we're also given an opportunity to reinvent ourselves. Each moment! This changing self can be reinvented to whatever we want. It's not completely tied to what it was a minute ago.

An example: a minute ago, I was someone who was procrastinating on writing this book. I could think, "Oh, what a horrible writer, what a procrastinator I am!" And feel horrible. Or I could let go of that image of myself, and instead reinvent myself as someone who is actually writing. I do that by starting to write.

So if you've been bad at habits, let go of that past self, because it's gone. Start a new self. And then a new one.

If your loved one has gotten angry at you, that feels bad. But that loved one's anger is caused by his or her suffering, and that suffering can be changed, can be eased. Your suffering as someone who has been wronged can also be changed. Instead, you can become a compassionate, empathetic person who gives comfort to this suffering loved one. You can let go of the wronged version of you, and become the calm, compassionate version of you. Your relationship can be healed, because it is constantly being reinvented.

This is not to say the past doesn't matter. It obviously affects the present and future. But we're not completely bound to the past—if everything is changing, that includes the harms and suffering of the past.

This might seem like heady stuff, and it is. We'll get into more concrete stuff soon, but it's good to see what we're up against as we deal with letting go. The skill of letting go helps us to deal with reality as it is, instead of how we'd like it to be, and be more skillful within that ever-changing reality.

Chapter 10

Dealing with Loss

One of the hardest things to deal with is a major loss, like the loss of a job, the loss of a house, the loss of a loved one who has died or is dying. But actually there are minor losses that we suffer from all the time: the loss of a contract, the loss of our health when we get a cold, the loss of who we thought we were when we suffer an embarrassment or failure.

These losses, big and small, cause us great suffering. And this suffering from loss is a part of life . . . but it doesn't have to be as great as it often is. We prolong the suffering out of habit.

Let's take a few examples:

- My favorite coffee mug breaks. This is a loss, and I feel sad or upset when it happens, naturally. But at this point, I could let it go and move on, and my suffering wouldn't be too bad. However, my habit might be to get mad at whoever broke the mug, and be resentful of them for awhile. Or if it just happened, I might ask, "Why did this happen to me?" And suffer for awhile, wishing the mug were whole again and the universe weren't so unfair to me. This prolonged suffering is caused by me, not the breaking of the mug. I'm holding onto what I wanted life to be (me having a great mug), not accepting what it is now.

- Amir loses his job. This of course is a big setback, and his life is now arguably much worse than before. And losing a job is a big blow to the ego, so Amir understandably suffers. But again, at this point, he can let go of the loss, accept his new reality (he's without a job), and now try to figure out what to do from here. Start applying to jobs, find a cheaper place to live, sell his car and get a bike, etc. Or he could be angry at the loss, and resentful and hurt. This continued suffering will hurt his job interviews, or perhaps even stop him from taking appropriate action. He might get into a fight with his girlfriend because he's so resentful. This prolonged suffering is caused by Amir, not the loss.

- Petra's husband Tomas leaves her and files for divorce. Petra, of course, is understandably hurt and angry at this betrayal of trust, this loss of her marriage and best friend. That's totally natural and there's nothing wrong with being hurt or angry—in fact, many people try to reject their feelings rather than accepting them, and this makes things worse. But after an initial reaction, she can choose to let go of what she was (a married woman with Tomas in her life) and accept her new reality (a single woman going through a divorce) and then take appropriate action, reinventing her life and herself. This can be liberating, this opportunity for reinvention. Or . . . she can dwell on the loss, on the betrayal, on the pain. Wish it were different. Ask why he doesn't love her. Stalk him on Facebook and hate his new girlfriend. Wallow in pity for months, eat to comfort herself, get overweight and unhealthy, never go out on dates because she's still stuck on Tomas and she doesn't like herself and she thinks her body is ugly. Okay, this is a bad scenario, but it does happen in various forms. Petra has hurt herself by not letting go.

- Justin's dad is dying of cancer. This is extremely painful for Justin, because he's already anticipating the pain of the loss of his father in less than a year. His anguish makes it difficult to help his father through this tough time, because instead of finding ways to help his father, he's focused on his own suffering. Instead of enjoying the time he has left with his father and appreciating his father right now in this moment, he's thinking ahead to what is going to happen, and can't let go of that dread. Instead, he can let go of this anticipated future, and of what he wished were true (he wishes his father weren't dying), and accept the situation and accept his own suffering. He can accept his dying father as the only father he has (there

is no healthy father anymore), and appreciate this new father right now. He can see the suffering his father must be going through, accept this suffering, and find compassion for his father in whatever ways he can. He can be grateful for each moment he has with his father, grateful for his own health, grateful for what his father has given him over the years.

And so while loss can be extremely difficult and painful, no matter how big or small the loss, we can prolong or shorten the suffering depending on whether we use the skill of letting go.

How can we let go after a loss? Well, we can accept our feelings about the loss, first of all. There's nothing wrong with being angry or sad at a loss. But after this mourning, we can see that we're holding onto something in the past, an idea of what we wish life still would be, instead of accepting how life is right now.

And this holding onto an idea of life, what we wish life were, is hurting us.

Seeing the harm allows us to let go, because we have a choice: hold on to the idea of the past and suffer, or let go and accept reality as it is, and suffer less.

We can then turn our attention on reality, as it is, and see the good in it. Appreciate what we have in front of us. See the opportunity for reinvention. Find compassion for ourselves and those around us who might also be suffering from this loss or other losses. Embrace the new life we have, for it is all we have.

This is the skill of letting go, and it helps tremendously with any kind of loss.

Chapter 11

Developing the Letting Go Skill

So we can see some of the benefits of letting go, and we can start to see how it might work. This is all great, but how do we actually develop the skill? It doesn't just happen with a snap of the fingers.

Instead, we must practice the skill of letting go.

And to practice a skill, it helps to break it down into smaller skills and examine those one at a time, practice them one at a time, before bringing them together into a larger skill.

A dancer, for example, might work on various steps of a complex dance move before putting them together and doing the entire move. That's what we're going to do with the letting go skill: break it into pieces and practice each piece, each mini-skill. And then bring it back together as a whole.

Here are the pieces:

1. **Noticing Signals:** When you are holding onto something that is harmful, it shows up in various little signals, symptoms like anger or procrastination. Seeing those signals as they happen is the first mini-skill.

2. **Seeing the Ideal:** What ideal are you holding onto that is causing the signal?

3. **Seeing the Harm:** Is the ideal causing you to suffer, harming your relationship, keeping you from being happy?

4. **Letting Go with Love:** If the ideal is causing harm, then letting go is an act of love and compassion.

5. **Seeing Reality:** Now that you've let go of an ideal, turn your attention to reality and see it as it is. Accept this, and respond appropriately.

Those all come together into the skill of letting go. The practice doesn't end there . . . there's still the question of how to act after you've let go. And we'll discuss that as well.

But first, let's examine the smaller skills, and then talk about how to practice them all and develop the habit of letting go.

Chapter 12

The 1st Skill: Noticing Signals

The first skill is noticing when you're holding onto something harmful—some kind of signal will appear, a sign that you're suffering.

These are the signals that you should practice the skill of letting go.

What are some of the signals? There are many, but here are some common ones:

- Anger

- Irritation

- Frustration

- Stress/anxiety

- Depression

- Jealousy

- Feeling hurt

- Wanting to be right

- Lashing out at someone

- Procrastination

- Wishing things were different

- Feeling insulted

- Wanting to get justice

- Angry driving

There is absolutely nothing wrong with feeling any of these things. We can't stop feeling them, and not wanting to feel them actually makes the suffering worse. So the first thing to know is that it's okay to feel these things, and that we should just feel them, accept them.

However, they are signals that something is going on. So after we've allowed ourselves to feel the feeling, we can pause before lashing out or taking an action we might regret. We can start the process of letting go, so that we don't prolong our suffering.

How do we practice this first skill, of noticing the signals? It's a learning process, but the first step is just to make a commitment to trying to notice when these things come up. It might surprise you, if you watch your-self, how often you feel a little bit of irritation or frustra-tion or anger, especially if you're around other people.

Just start noticing. You don't have to do the other steps yet—just practice noticing for a few days or so, until you get pretty good at it.

Chapter 13

The 2nd Skill: Seeing the Ideal

Now that you've noticed the signal, the next part of the process is to turn inward and see what's causing this signal, this symptom.

It didn't just happen randomly—there's a cause of the signal. If you're angry, it's not just someone else's fault. They did something, perhaps, but that's just an occurrence in the outside world around you, like a leaf falling or the wind blowing or a rock falling off a cliff. They just happen, but your anger comes not from the occurrence but because you don't want the thing to occur.

It's your not wanting what has happened to have happened, or your not wanting the way things are to be the way they are, that's causing the anger or frustration.

Imagine if you were just a camera, recording what's going on, neutrally and without any desires for things to be a certain way, or people to act a certain way. In this case, if someone does something, you wouldn't get angry, because you're a neutral observation tool, without any preferences for what happens in the world.

Of course, in reality, you're not a camera. You have expectations of others, ideals for yourself, ideals of how the world should be. And it's these ideals/expectations that cause the anger and frustration.

These ideals and expectations aren't reality—if they matched reality, you wouldn't be angry. They are your fantasies of what reality should be. The fantasies aren't reality, and they're causing the anger.

So turn inward for a minute: What ideal are you holding onto that is causing the signal?

Sometimes it can be hard to see what ideal you have, but if you practice this for awhile, you'll get better at it.

Just a few ideals you might have:

1. People should be considerate.

2. People should be fair.

3. People should respect you and not insult you.

4. People should be positive and not complain or be moody.

5. You'll be successful at what you do.

6. You'll be comfortable and do easy things.

7. Your life will be full of joy and pleasures and no pains.

8. You'll be good at changing habits.

9. People on the road or sidewalk won't get in your way.

10. Things will be where you need them.

11. Your home will be neat and people working and living with you will always be neat.

12. Your kids will do exactly as you say.

13. Your spouse or friends will be enthusiastic and supportive of all your ideas.

14. People will immediately see your brilliance and want to hire you.

15. Loved ones won't go away or die.

16. People you love will love you back exactly the same as you love them.

This is just a start—there are hundreds and perhaps thousands of ideals that we have at various times. We can identify them because when someone violates them, or life doesn't meet them, we aren't happy. So our ideal is the opposite of what has happened.

After practicing noticing the signals for awhile, start to turn inward and notice what your ideal is that's causing the signal. Practice until the ideal becomes easy to see.

Chapter 14

The 3rd Skill: Seeing the Harm

You've noticed the signal, and now you're able to see the ideal that's causing the signal. But what's wrong with having anger or frustration or jealousy or hurt feelings? Isn't that part of being human?

Yes, it's absolutely a part of the human experience, and there's nothing wrong with feeling them. However, acting on these feelings and holding onto them can cause us to be unhappy, prolong our stress until it grows to unhealthy levels, harm our relationships by causing us to resent people in our lives, even harm our relationship with ourselves because we similarly get angry or frustrated with ourselves, holding ourselves up to ideals.

So feelings are not bad, nor is having ideals—they're a natural part of our human experience. But if the ideals are causing harm to ourselves and the people around us, the perhaps we can let go of them.

If the ideals are causing us to do good in the world, then we don't need to let go of them. An ideal might cause us to be compassionate or generous, for example. There's nothing wrong with having ideals—in fact, I don't think we can avoid having them.

It's when the ideal is harming us or others that we would benefit from letting the go.

And so as you notice the signal, and the ideal that's causing it, ask yourself if it's causing you or others harm. In the case of anger or other types of unhappiness, it's almost certain that it's causing harm.

When you notice the harm it's causing, then letting go is a compassionate act. It's an act of ending suffering. Letting go can be a painful thing—after all, these ideals are often a big part of who we are and of our worldview. But the pain of letting go is often very little compared to the benefits of letting go of something that is harming us or people around us.

Practice seeing the harm, when you notice the signal and the ideal.

You'll get good at this in no time.

Chapter 15

The 4th Skill: Letting Go with Love

So letting go can be a compassionate act, if the ideal is causing harm.

Here's how to let go with compassion and love:

First, wish yourself and others around you happiness.

See that the ideal is causing suffering.

Want to end that suffering by letting go of the ideal.

If you don't want to let go of the ideal, instead of focusing on wanting the ideal, focus on how good things would be if you didn't have it.

Let your heart and mind relax, so that you can let the ideal float away. The tightened chest loosens a bit, you breathe a little deeper, a warm feeling of love grows inside you, and you let go of whatever you've tightened around

You are now a new person, with one less ideal (for the moment anyway—ideals can and often do come back later). This person is different than the person you were, which means you can reinvent this person, make this person calm and compassionate.

Be this new person.

Once you've let go of the ideal (which takes practice—more on this in a bit), the question is, now what? We'll look at that in the next chapter (Seeing Reality) and Chapter 18 (How to Act After Letting Go).

Chapter 16

The 5th Skill: Seeing Reality

Let's say you successfully let go. That's not always easy, and you'll practice that skill in the next chapter . . . but let's say you did let go.

It's now time to turn your attention to reality and see it as it is. Accept this, and respond appropriately.

Let's say you are disappointed with your son for not behaving as you'd like, not living up to your expectations. You see that this disappointment and your ideal are causing you harm, so you try letting go of the ideal. And now, you turn to your son and just try to see him as he is. He's a good person, with hopes and a desire to be happy, and he's suffering and uncertain how to act in a chaotic world. This is the reality of your son.

You can reject this, or accept him as he is. Try to be compassionate with him if he's suffering. Try to be grateful for who he is. Just be with him and be happy that you get to be with him.

There's a lot you can do once you see him as he is, but you have to first turn to him as see what's there.

This is true not only with other people, but with yourself. Instead of measuring yourself against your ideals of what you should be, see yourself as you really are.

And it is true with life all around you: it's not what your ideals say it should be. But it's pretty great, just as it is.

Turn the power of your attention to reality, and really try to see it, just as it is. There's more to do after this, but let's practice these five mini-skills first.

Chapter 17

Practicing the Skills

We have five mini-skills that we're going to practice and put together into one big skill, one healing process.

Here are my recommendations for practicing:

1. **First, make a commitment to practice just a few minutes a day.** You won't practice consistently without a very strong commitment. But this is an easy commitment—it won't take a lot of time, and you'll easily be able to practice if you can remember. Make the commitment because this matters—it will help you be happier, deal with change better, procrastinate less, have better relationships, deal with change. Make a commitment to others—a loved one, an accountability partner. A commitment to yourself is great, but if you're going to take it seriously, make a commitment to someone else to practice daily.

2. **Set aside some practice time.** Just a few minutes in the morning or evening, or at lunch. Set aside a specific time, or you won't practice.

3. **Have reminders.** You'll forget to practice. So put a sticky note on your laptop, create calendar reminders, phone reminders, ask your accountability partner to remind you. Put up a physical note somewhere you will see it. This is incredibly important—most people skip this step and never practice their new habit.

4. **Sit and practice daily.** Start tomorrow, just 2–3 minutes. Tell your accountability partner or group when you're done. Here's the practice . . . think about some signs you've had recently that you're holding onto something. For a few days at least, just try to remember as many of those signs as possible from the last day or so. Then, when you get better at this, try to see the ideal you're holding onto that are causing the signs. Then after a few more days, practice seeing the harm the ideals are causing. Then after a few more days, practice letting go of the ideal with

love and compassion. Then after yet a few more days, practice seeing things or people as they really are.

You don't need to practice one skill at a time if they're coming easy to you. If you can easy see the signs and the ideals and the harm, then practice the letting go immediately.

Further practice: Once you've gotten pretty good at the above practice, try this in your daily session:

Consider that you're going to die someday. Everyone around you is going to die. The plants and animals around you are also going to die. Every object in your home will someday break or rot. This is the natural process of life—it's constantly changing, and in the place of the old stuff, new stuff is being created. Everything is impermanent. See everything changing, dying, breaking, and being created.

Now consider the futility in trying to keep anything the same. See how everything is temporary, and wanting it to be permanent will only cause you to suffer. See how you not wanting things to die doesn't stop them from dying—but you feel anxiety because you wish things weren't the way they were. And then see how letting go of that wishing, and accepting the changing nature of things, and being unattached to each moment of those changing things, will help you to be calmer and happier. Embrace the non-attachment. Embrace the changing nature of things as beautiful. Accept the impermanence.

Still further practice: This daily letting go session is just the start. Once you get decent at each step, make a commitment to seeing the signs as they happen, during the day, not just during the session.

You can skip to this practice if all of this comes easy to you.

When you see the signs as they happen easily, practice the other steps. After awhile, you'll get good at doing this process in the moment, especially when the stakes aren't too high. When your emotions are running high, it can be very difficult to practice letting go, so it's best to just feel the emotion but try not to react until you've had a chance to calm down and practice letting go.

If you have difficulty letting go: Often the letting go part of the process can be very difficult. Here's what I suggest:

- Practice with easy things first: Practice letting go of possessions you don't care about.

- Do it in small doses: Practice letting go of an ideal like a clean house just for a day, not forever.

- Practice with people you don't have difficulty with: If there's a co-worker or relative you have a troubled relationship with, it can be difficult to let go of things. Practice with people you have a better relationship with, as this is an easier practice.

- Practice letting go of a desire, like buying something or drinking a little wine, for just five minutes.

Then practice for another five minutes. Then let yourself have it.

- Practice letting go of distractions, for just 10 minutes at a time. Sit there with an important task, like writing something, and don't let yourself go to distractions. Let go of the distractions temporarily, seeing the ideal (probably wanting things to be easy and comfortable) and how it's harming you.

Improving practice: If you find yourself forgetting to practice or find your practice faltering, there are some things you can do to get better:

- Report daily to an accountability partner. Email each other with notes on your practice. Or journal and share your journal twice a week.

- Plan your practice for the week. At the end of the week, review how well you followed the plan, and what obstacles stopped you from following the plan. What can you do to overcome those obstacles in the future? Improve your plan next week by adding these techniques to overcome your obstacles. If you stick to this process, you'll get better and better at the practice over time.

Chapter 18

How to Act After Letting Go

Letting go and seeing things as they really are . . . this isn't the end. There's now the question of how to act once you've let go and turned your attention to reality.

There are some good possibilities to practice:

- Accept this moment for what it is, be grateful for it, and enjoy it.

- Accept another person for who they are, and enjoy their company. Just be with them in acceptance.

- Accept yourself for who you are, and be content with yourself.

- See that someone else (or yourself) is acting this way because they are suffering, and try to be compassionate with them.

- See that there's a legitimate problem to be solved, other than the anger you're both feeling (which is just a symptom). But letting go of the ideal and the anger helps you and the other person to solve the problem more calmly and compassionately.

- Let go of the ideal, see reality as it is, and respond appropriately. Without taking anything personally. Just respond to reality.

- Just be in reality as it is, without judgment. Just be, don't try to solve a problem or achieve anything, for a little while.

- Let go of controlling things and just let them happen for a bit, being in the moment as they happen without trying to control things.

- See the impermanent nature of reality . . . watch it change and flow each moment. This is a fascinating and enlightening learning process.

There are other possibilities, of course, but these are a few prompts to think about as you decide how to act once you've let go.

Chapter 19

What Letting Go Isn't

There are a lot of misconceptions about and objections to the idea of letting go, mostly because it's in such opposition to our normal way of thinking. We're used to trying to control things, trying to make things happen, trying to fight for justice and how things should be, trying to get people to act considerately and with fairness, trying to make the world and ourselves better all the time.

Accepting isn't part of this worldview. Letting go isn't part of the worldview.

But compassion and love and pain and anger are all part of the worldview, so we should see letting go and accepting as tools to deal with those feelings.

What letting go isn't:

1. **Letting go isn't about giving up.** Let's say you're

having a fight—letting go of an ideal feels like you're giving up and letting someone else win. But actually the fight isn't about winning, it's about solving a problem and making the relationship better. If you can let go of what's causing you to be angry, you can talk more calmly and compassionately, and instead have a sane talk about what went wrong (not who's to blame) and how to fix the problem. You can even talk about feelings, compassionately, without letting anger lash out at the other person. It's not about giving up, but about solving the problem appropriately.

2. **Letting go isn't about being a victim.** If someone did something bad to you, that's horrible of course. And of course you'd be hurt and angry and feel violated. There's nothing wrong with feeling these things, and in fact you should let yourself feel them. But there's often a desire to get revenge, which is harmful both to you and the other person. And while it might feel good to try to harm the other person, that doesn't actually make things better.

It doesn't really make you happier. And what happens if you can't actually hurt the other person for some reason? You don't get that satisfaction. Either way, you continue to suffer much longer. If instead you can let go of the suffering (after allowing yourself to feel the pain for awhile), you can begin to heal. That's the most important thing—not revenge. Healing allows you to be happy, rather than suffering for the other person's crime for the rest of your life.

1. **Letting go isn't about not improving.** Lots of people think they need ideals to improve their lives, improve themselves . . . and that letting go of ideals means not improving. First, if the ideal is helping you, there's no need to let go of it, but if it's harming you then you should try letting go, even if that's difficult. Second, you really only need "improvement" if you don't think you're good enough right now . . . and in truth, you already have everything you need to be happy right now. You are good enough, if you can learn to let go of the ideals you've set for yourself and accept yourself as you are. There is wonder in who you already are. Now, once you've accepted yourself, you can still create new habits, not to try to improve yourself to some ideal, but because it's a compassionate act for yourself or others.

2. **Letting go isn't about letting someone else get away with something.** Yes, other people behave badly, and yes you'll want to make them pay or correct them. But if you go around trying to mete out justice in this world, you'll always be angry, and you won't actually change people. People don't change because you yell at them. They might

change if you let go of your anger and compassionately talk to them about the problem. Or maybe not, but either way, you've let go of your anger and you're happier.

3. **Letting go isn't about letting your house get messy.** If you have an ideal of how your house should look (or something else similar), you might get frustrated or angry when other people don't help you keep the house clean. Then you'll resent them, perhaps lash out at them in some way. This doesn't make you happy and isn't good for your relationship with them. But does that mean you should unfairly have to do all the cleaning, or that you should just let the house become a complete dump? Not necessarily. First, if you can let go of the ideal of everyone keeping the house clean, you can let go of your anger and resentment. This allows you to be calmer and accept people for who they are (and see that they're suffering, and that they don't have good habits in place to support your ideal). Seeing people as they are helps you to have a better relationship with them, but also to calmly and compassionately talk to them about how to solve the problem. If they don't want to solve the problem, then what? Well, you can accept that you can't control people, and instead focus on what you can control. Which can be frustrating, only if you think you should be able to control other people. You might come up with an

agreement for the house that you can all agree to. You might move out eventually if your roommates aren't acceptable. Most effective of all is setting an example to see if that has an influence on them. And continue to talk to them (calmly) about your feelings about the house, and hope that you can come to a resolution to your dispute. However you do it, you're doing it without the resentment and anger.

4. **Letting go isn't about not making the world a better place.** Making the world a better place is great, but when your ideals about how the world should be (that everyone should behave perfectly and work in unison toward the solutions you want) are causing you to suffer, then it's time to loosen your hold on them. Accept that the world isn't ideal, but that it's great as it is. And also see that once you've calmed down and accepted the world as it is, you can still see people's suffering and act out of compassion to make people's lives better.

5. **Letting go isn't about letting the other person be right when they're wrong.** Often one of the greatest sources of frustration is wanting to show others that we're right, and they're wrong. This causes us to be angry and insistent, and causes others to be the same way. This makes us all unhappy and damages our relationships. Instead, we

can let go of the ideal of being right, and instead accept that we have a disagreement. How can we calmly and compassionately respond to this disagreement? Is it important to shove your rightness into the other person's mind? Or have a good relationship, and work out the best way forward?

6. **Letting go isn't about giving up standards of common decency in our society.** People should treat each other with consideration and respect. People should be fair and not cut each other off in traffic. These are some standards we have in society—so is letting go of them an abandonment of those standards? No . . . it's letting go of the ideal that everyone will live up to those standards all the time. In reality, many people will live up to the standards, and many will violate it. They are probably suffering in some way, which doesn't excuse the misbehavior but it can help us to empathize and work with them compassionately. And help us forgive. We can perhaps educate them about the standard, but often not, and if not we can let go of our frustration. We can have group discussions about the standards and agree to them, but also know that standards will not be completely lived up to, ever. And that's okay.

There are lots of other things letting go isn't as well,

but you can see the common thread: it starts with letting go and accepting reality, so that we can respond appropriately and not suffer more than we need to.

And that's such a huge change from how most of us operate on a daily basis that it's worth a little practice.

Chapter 20

Examples of Letting Go

So what does letting go look like in daily life? Let's take a look at some examples of what you might do in different situations with the practice.

- **Your co-worker is rude to you.** Your initial reaction might be anger or feeling offended, because you're holding onto an ideal of how people should treat you. The anger will only make the situation worse, though, and you'll be angry and unhappy. So you practice putting aside the ideal and anger, and instead try to see the suffering the co-worker must be going through in order to act this way. Either he's suffering especially today and lashing out at you (he's not handling his problems well) or he does this habitually which means he's suffering throughout his life. You can empathize with suffering, as you do it yourself, and you've also lashed out at people before so you know that's a very human mistake. Seeing this suffering, empathizing with it, you can respond appropriately, seeing if you can ease the suffering. Later, when he's calmed down, you can try expressing in a compassionate way that you felt you were treated rudely and try to work with him to find a better way for you both to express your frustrations.

- **Your son doesn't clean his room.** You're frustrated/angry because your son is supposed to behave differently—he's being inconsiderate, you've told him a thousand times, etc. Your anger is not caused by your son, but by your ideal of how he should behave. His actions don't meet your ideal, so you're frustrated. This anger hurts your relationship with him, because you lash out and show him how unhappy you are with him, and he gets defensive and tired of you lashing out, understandably. Plus you're not happy. So you practice setting aside your ideal for now, calm down, and see your son for who he is: a good person, wanting to be happy, who doesn't have the right habits (neither do you) or perhaps has different priorities than you. His way of being happy is different than yours. So you appreciate him for who he is, go and see what makes him happy, give him a hug, spend time with him as you accept him for who he is. And if there's an issue with his cleaning habits, maybe you could both calmly talk it out and find a solution that

works for both of you, recognizing that he'll probably mess up in this habit and just needs to be
supported by you in creating new habits.

- **Your daughter throws a tantrum.** She's not behaving according to your ideal of a perfect child,
and so you're frustrated. You blow up, act out of
anger, which hurts you and her. Or instead, you
set aside your ideal of the perfect way for her
to behave, and accept her "bad" behavior. And
then see that actually, she's frustrated and this
is the only way she knows to behave when she's
frustrated. She's dealing with the same letting
go issues you are! And handling it badly. So you
can 1) see her suffering, 2) comfort her in her
suffering, and 3) start to calmly teach her better
ways to better ways to deal with her frustration,
when she's calmed down. But realize that how
you deal with your frustration is really what she'll
learn, not what you say to her. So lead by example
by letting go and putting your frustration aside,
and she'll learn from that example.

- **Your father is dying of cancer.** This is understandably extremely sad, and you immediately
feel the loss and grief. And you feel it for months,
as he's dying. You wish he were better. You wish he
weren't going to die. These are ideals (a healthy
father, one who isn't going to die) that of course
aren't in line with reality. So what can you do?

Practice letting go of these ideals, and accept your father for who he is right now (someone dying), also accepting your suffering and his. Be with him, in acceptance, and just appreciate him as he is. Be grateful for your time with him, and for all he's given you. Be compassionate with him, trying to help him through his suffering. Reflect on the nature of your own life, and see that you don't have much time left, and decide how you want to spend that time you have—by wishing things were different and suffering, or by building relationships, finding happiness, making others happy.

- **Your wife seems distant and uninterested in you.** You are frustrated or hurt because she's not meeting your ideal of how she should act (with love and warmness and caring, all the time). This makes you act badly, hurting the relationship more, and makes you unhappy. Instead, try letting go of how she should act, and see her as she is: suffering. She's going through something, and perhaps you can be compassionate with her. Perhaps she'll want to talk to you about it, or perhaps she wants space. Imagine a time when you wanted space to go through something on your own. Realize it's not about you, but something she's going through. But when things are calm, you should definitely have a talk with her about what's going on and how the two of you can find a solution together.

- **You have too much to do today.** This causes you anxiety/stress, because your ideal is having just the right amount to do, and that you'll do it all well, with calm and happiness. The stress causes you to have a bad day, and perhaps to do some of what you're doing badly, because you can't completely focus due to the stress. Instead, try putting aside your ideal. Accept your suffering, comfort yourself. Accept the situation: you have a ton of work, and limited time. Use the limited time wisely by doing one thing at a time, as best you can given your time limitations, then do the next thing. Renegotiate demands if it becomes obvious that you aren't going to meet deadlines. You can't do more than one thing at a time, so get focused, get your work done, and accept your limitations. And actually, if you practice this one task at a time method, you can learn to work with focus and calm, and be happy in your work.

- **You want to exercise but keep putting it off.** You aren't living up to your ideals about how disciplined you're going to be, and it frustrates you and makes you feel bad about yourself. You comfort yourself, because you're feeling bad, with food and TV. This only makes you feel worse over the long run, because you can't get your act together. Instead, let go of the ideal of how disciplined you should be. Accept that you're suffering, that you have a lot to do and are tired and this makes you want to procrastinate on exercise. Have compassion for this suffering. And see the exercise as a compassionate way to relieve the suffering—it relieves stress, makes you feel better about yourself. Leave behind bad feelings about your past failures, figure out a better plan for exercising that will help you overcome your obstacles (sleep earlier if you're tired, exercise at lunch if you can't do it after work, etc.). Be in the moment with the exercise rather than wanting the exercise to be what it's not (easy and comfortable).

- **You've been waiting for a visa to be ready by today so you can travel, but it's not going to be done until next week.** This is going to ruin your planned trip! It's incredibly frustrating, because you've been fantasizing about this trip for two months, you've made plans with friends, you have a big meeting there, and now you'll have to let everyone down. Life isn't meeting your ideal of everything going perfectly, you having the perfect trip, not letting anyone down. So you're super frustrated, angry at the visa office, wishing things were different. Your anger doesn't make the visa come any faster, it just makes you unhappy. Instead, let go of your ideal—it doesn't exist in reality and isn't going to. It's only causing you unhappiness. Turn to your suffering, accept it, comfort it. Accept that this trip isn't happening as planned. Tell people that things have changed.

Figure out a new plan based on the reality of the new circumstances. See that this new reality isn't really worse than what you'd hoped for, but is only worse if you compare it with your fantasy. Life isn't your fantasy, so dropping the fantasy and appreciating the reality will help you greatly.

- **You are unhappy about your body.** Your body doesn't meet your ideals for what it should look like—lean, with great breasts or muscles or whatever. So you feel unhappy with yourself, and to comfort this unhappiness perhaps you eat, and make things worse. Your ideal is causing you unhappiness. Instead, put the ideal away for a bit. It's just a fantasy. Accept the reality of your body— it's actually great as it is, if you can learn to see the greatness in it. Imagine all the amazing things it can do! Think of how it serves you every day. Wow! What a great body. Okay, it doesn't meet the image of a cover model, but that's just fantasy designed to get you to buy a magazine or clothes. Instead, be compassionate with your suffering. Accept that you're overweight, and calmly figure out what you can do to get healthier. You'll never get to an ideal body (that's fantasy) but you can 1) learn to be grateful for your body as it is, and 2) focus on health. Do healthy things, like eating vegetables and less junk, exercising and meditating. That's more productive than comparing your body to a fantasy.

There are obviously dozens more examples I could write, but if you read the above examples carefully, you'll see a pattern that emerges, and you'll be able to apply the pattern to any situation:

1. See how the ideal is making you suffer.

2. See how the ideal is making the situation worse (you being angry only hurts your relationship, you being unhappy causes you to comfort yourself with food, etc.).

3. Try putting aside your ideal and anger.

4. Turn to your suffering, accept the suffering, and comfort yourself.

5. See the other person or the situation as it really is. See that the other person is suffering too. Accept the other person as they are, accept the situation as it is.

6. Give the other person compassion.

7. Deal calmly with the situation appropriately. Find ways to make the situation better if there's a problem to be solved. Be grateful for things as they are.

Of course, you won't always meet this ideal pattern. You'll handle things badly, as we all do. And that's okay. See what happened, in retrospect, and see how you could have done it differently, how using the pattern above might have helped. Then try practicing that next time.

Chapter 21

Where to Go Next

You've come to the end of this book, but this might just be the start of the journey.

That depends on you.

Will you nod your head at this book, and say "interesting ideas" and then go on with your life as before?

Or will you make a commitment to practicing letting go, and see if it has any benefits in your life?

My hypothesis is that if you practice letting go, you'll find yourself less angry and irritated and frustrated. You'll wish things were different less, wonder less often why you have to suffer, be more present.

But this is only a hypothesis. We won't really know until you test it out.

Test it out for a few weeks. Commit to someone else. Commit to a daily practice of 2–3 minutes. Set up reminders.

Sit for a few minutes, and practice.

See what happens.

Then let me know: Letting Go Results

You can let me know how it went, or if you have questions or obstacles you'd like to report.

It would really help me out.

Thanks for reading this, my friends. Enjoy the journey.

Leo Babauta
Zen Habits

About the Author

Leo Babauta is the creator of Zen Habits, a blog about simplicity, habits and mindfulness. He lives in San Francisco with his wife and six kids.

Leo started his journey in changing his life in 2005, when he quit smoking and then took up running. Over the course of the next year or so, he ran a marathon, lost 30+ lbs. (and eventually 70 lbs.), became vegetarian and then later vegan, reduced and then eliminated his debt, started waking earlier, procrastinating less, and got rid of all his clutter.

He started Zen Habits to share what he learned in changing a few dozen habits, and today helps people change their lives through his books and his Sea Change habit program.